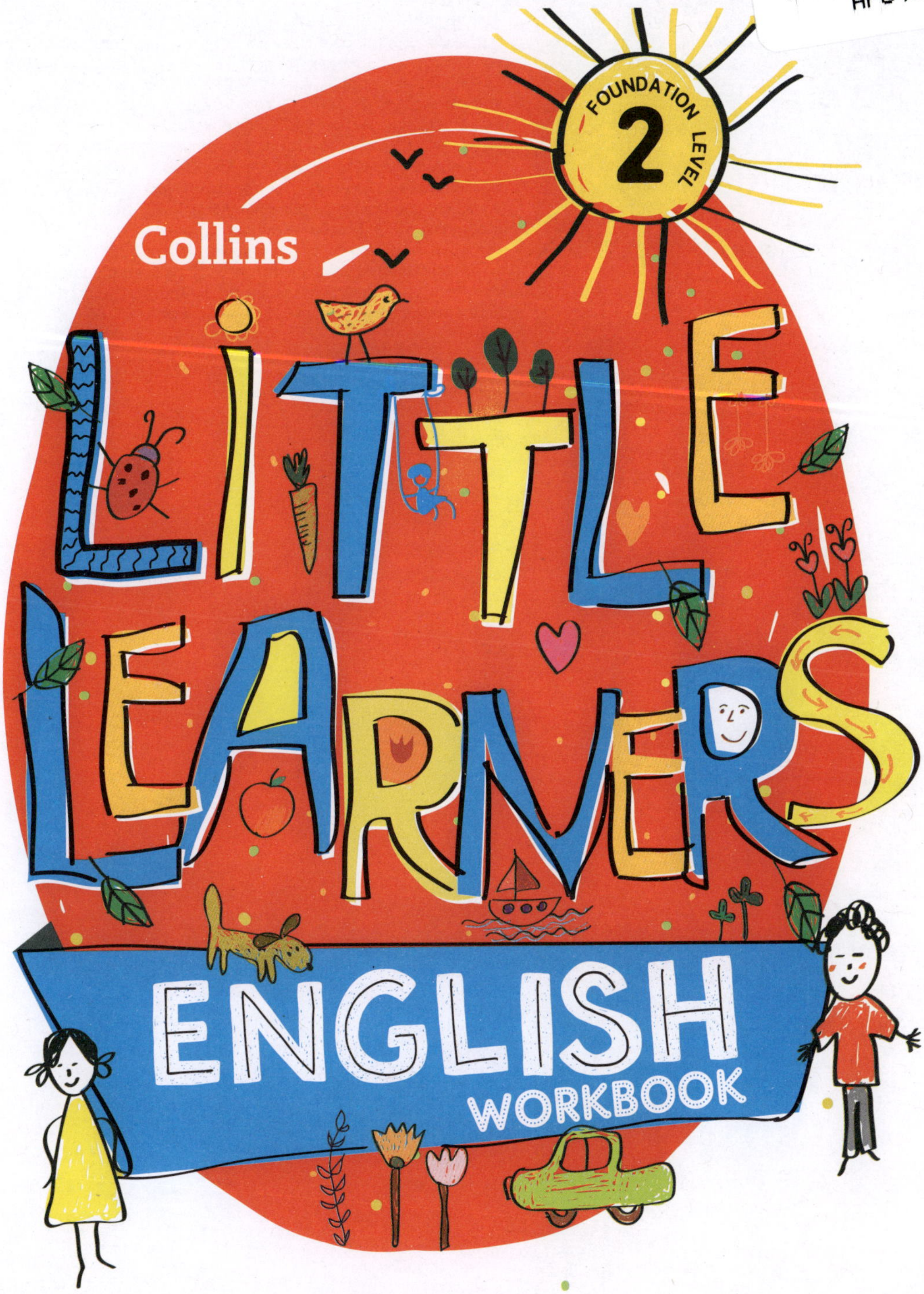

LITTLE LEARNERS ENGLISH

WORKBOOK

SERIES EDITOR: RANI T.

Published by Collins Learning
A division of HarperCollins*Publishers*
India Private Limited

HarperCollins Publishers
Building No 10, Tower A, 4th Floor,
DLF Cyber City, Phase II, Gurgaon 122002

1 London Bridge Street, London, SE1 9GF,
United Kingdom

2 Bloor Street East, Toronto, Ontario M4W 1A8, Canada

Lvl 13, 201 Elizabeth Street (PO Box A565, NSW, 1235), Sydney NSW 2000, Australia

195 Broadway, New York, NY 10007, USA

Browse the complete Collins catalogue at www.collins.in
For any queries/feedback, please write to us at **SCHOOLSUPPORT@harpercollins.co.in** or call us on 0124-4894800.

First published in 2020

Reprint: 10 9 8 7 6 5 4 3 2 1

ISBN: 978-935357-040-8

Layout and Artwork by
Typeface Printographics Pvt. Ltd.

Printed and bound by
MicroPrints India, New Delhi

Acknowledgements

Cover: HarperCollins*Publishers*India

Title Page: HarperCollins*Publishers*India

Prelim Pages: radenmas, denkcreative, nonohana, graphic-bee

Inside: pg 14: 7romawka7; pg 15: neyro2008; pg 16: graphic-bee; pg 17: art-sonik, Dar_ria; pg 18: Tomacco; pg 19: Betsart, pleshko74; pg 22: StudioBarcelona, nyamol; pg 23: artbesouro, ikryannikovgmailcom; pg 24: RobinOlimb, Mochipet; pg 25: Kittisak_Taramas, Naveed Anjum; pg 26: VectorMoon, S-S-S; pg 29: Naddiya, Vectorpower; pg 30: SIlviaCV, IconicBestiary; pg 31: blueringmedia, lemur4eg; pg 32: lishenjun, HitToon; pg 33: graphic-bee, Vectorpower, nyamol, Naveed Anjum; pg 37: MariaTkach, saenal78; pg 38: IconicBestiary, blueringmedia; pg 39: kontur-vid, pijama61; pg 40: blueringmedia, aekikuis; pg 41: jehsomwang, Tarchyshnik; pg 44: Nikiteev_Konstantin, Tetiana Lazunova; pg 45: Jenyk, pijama61; pg 46: Tetiana Lazunova, blueringmedia; pg 47: luplupme, Usagi-D; pg 48: pleshko74, drogatnev; pg 49: Nosyrevy, luplupme; pg 51: StudioBarcelona, kontur-vid; Tetiana Lazunova; pg 52: pleshko74, art-sonik, Jenyk; pg 53: saenal78, artbesouro; pg 54: Mochipet, Naveed Anjum, aekikuis; pg 55: luplupme, Tarchyshnik; pg 56: S-S-S, Vectorpower, SIlviaCV, blueringmedia, HitToon; pg 58: ikryannikovgmailcom, aekikuis, luplupme; pg 59: Vectorpower, blueringmedia, HitToon.

Preface

Collins Little Learners, comprising 20 books in all, provides graded, age-appropriate learning opportunities targeting holistic skill development for children in the age group of 3 years to 6 years. Spread across three levels, the series spans **English**, **Maths**, **General Awareness**, **Art and Craft** and **Hindi**. The series comes bundled with a **workbook** for English and a book of **rhymes and stories** for each level. The books use a combination of hands-on activities, frequent recapitulation and child-friendly artwork to facilitate learning.

The early years are the most significant years for growth, development and learning. During this period, children need adequate opportunities for stimulating experiences as these favourably affect various learning abilities. Learning experiences, when chosen and planned properly, fuel the innate curiosity of children, and stimulate their thought processes.

Learning and Development During the Early Years

The goal of learning during the early years is to enhance the all-round development of personality and to inculcate healthy attitudes, life skills and good values. Creative play, well thought-out games and developmentally appropriate activities help children develop the necessary skills to achieve these goals. The skills that children need to acquire can broadly be categorized as:

Motor: Motor skills pertain not only to gross motor activities like walking and jumping but also include fine motor activities like the ability to hold a pencil and write. The development of motor skills is facilitated through several graded activities.

Personal, Social and Emotional: Personal, social and emotional development, necessary for the overall personality development of children, is achieved using a combination of hands-on activities, role plays, and thought-provoking stories and rhymes.

Linguistic: The ability to listen, speak, read and write is critical to success in formal learning environments.

Mathematical: The development of mathematical ideas and concepts is important at this stage since children will continue to build on this learning for most of their years of schooling.

Knowledge and Understanding of the World: This is achieved through activities that enable children to explore their surroundings at home and in the school, and interact with the people that they see around them.

Health and Safety: The idea of health and safety is introduced through activities, stories and retelling of real-life experiences to encourage children to focus on health and well-being.

Creative: Creative skills are developed through a host of activities involving art, craft, painting, roleplays, etc.

Logical and Rational Thinking: Activities that involve simple puzzles, pattern-completion and visual discrimination help children develop logical and rational thinking skills.

The Collins Little Learners Teacher Support Materials

The series includes extensive teacher support in the form of:

Teacher's Resource Books: Comprises stories, activity banks, classroom management and assessment guidelines

Multimedia eBook: Consists of animations, audio, video, slide shows, and interactive exercises

Print-ready Worksheets: Additional worksheets for practice and reinforcement, present in the digital support

Digital Flashcards: Flashcards with embedded sounds and animations for letter formation and letter-sound association

Animations and Songs: Animated stories and rhymes set to tune

Interactive Games: Interactivities to reinforce concepts in a fun and engaging manner

A note on the activity banks (included in the Teacher's Manuals)

The activity banks comprise hands-on activities that will help children develop the requisite skills to attain age-appropriate learning goals. In keeping with Howard Gardener's theory of multiple intelligences, the activity banks include options and variations that enable teachers to provide a planned cycle of experiences and opportunities, which foster each type of intelligence, to every child in their classrooms. The activity banks equip teachers to use the strengths of children as a means of complementing their less developed areas by valuing and nurturing the inherent abilities of the children.

Contents

Fun Time!

Join the dots to complete the picture. Colour it.

I Know Letters Aa–Zz

Use crayons to trace the capital letters.

A a

B b

C c

D d

E e

F f

I Know Letters Aa–Zz

Use crayons to trace the capital letters.

G g

H h

I i

J j

K k

L l

I Know Letters Aa–Zz

Use crayons to trace the capital letters.

I Know Letters Aa–Zz

Use crayons to trace the capital letters.

Ss

Tt

Uu

Vv

Ww

Xx

I Know Letters Aa–Zz

Use crayons to trace the capital letters.

1 2 3 Y y

1 2 3 Z z

Match the capital letters to the small letters.

B •	• f
D •	• k
F •	• g
K •	• d
G •	• b

I Can Trace Patterns!

Trace the patterns.

Hello Letter T

Trace and write.

Trace

Hello Letter I

Trace and write.

Trace

Hello Letter L

Trace and write.

L

Trace

L L L L L

Hello Letter F

Trace and write.

F

Trace

F F F F F

Hello Letter H

Trace and write.

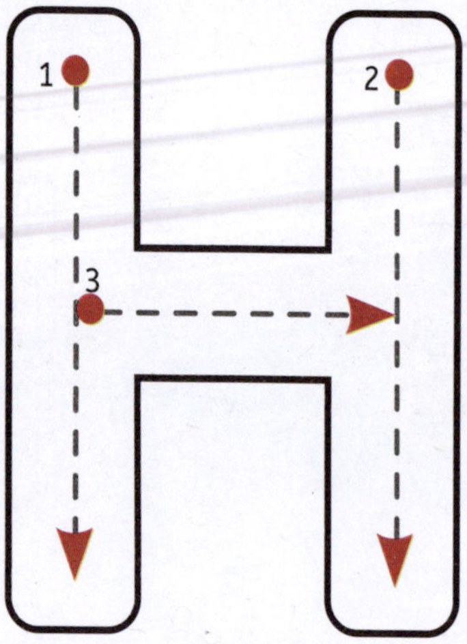

Trace

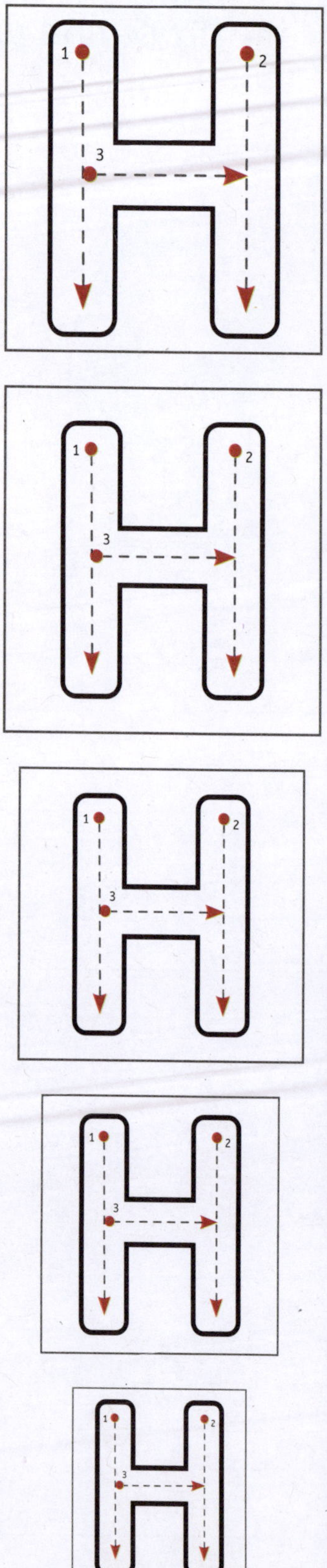

Hello Letter E

Trace and write.

Trace

I Can Write!

Trace the letters. Write them on your own.

T

I

L

F

H

E

I Can Trace Patterns!

Trace the patterns.

Hello Letter A

Trace and write.

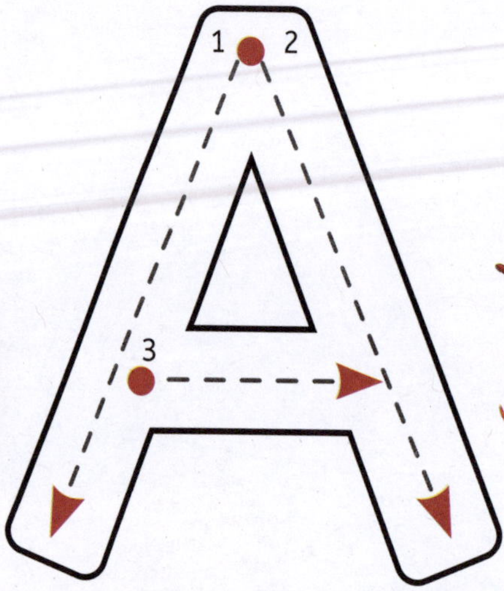

Trace

Hello Letter K

Trace and write.

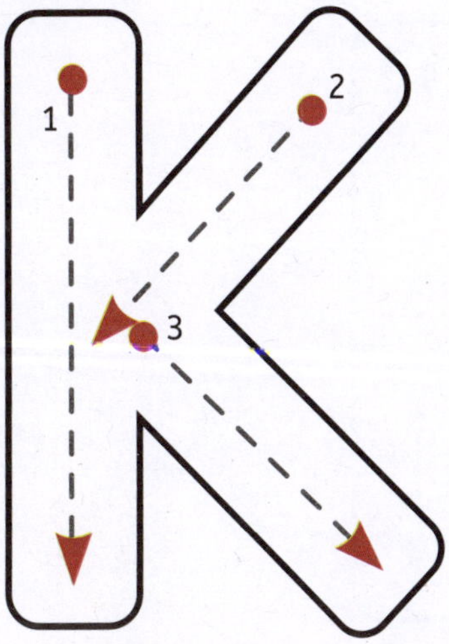

Trace

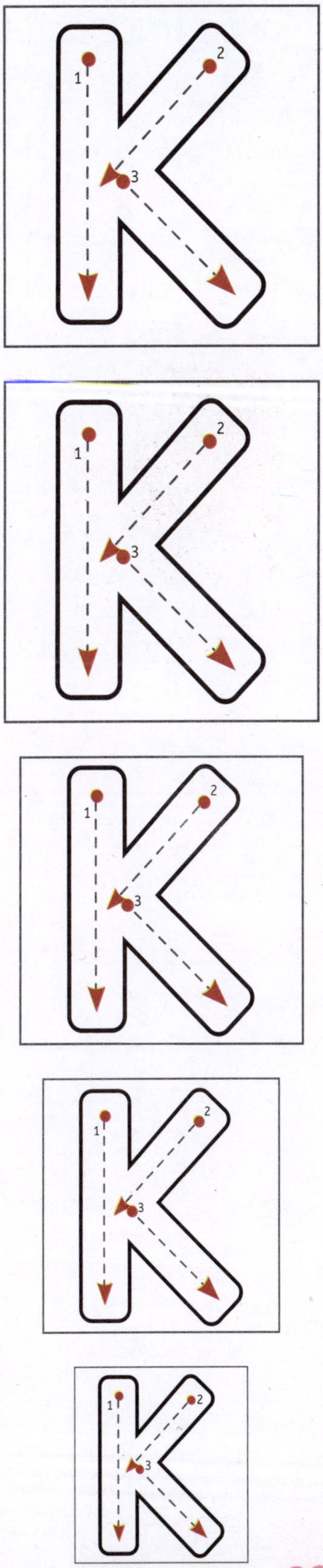

Hello Letter M

Trace and write.

M

M M M M M

M M M M M

Trace

M

M

M

M

M

Hello Letter N

Trace and write.

Trace

Hello Letter V

Trace and write.

Trace

I Can Write!

Trace the letters. Write them on your own.

A A

K K

M M

N N

V V

I Can Trace Patterns!

Trace the patterns.

Hello Letter W

Trace and write.

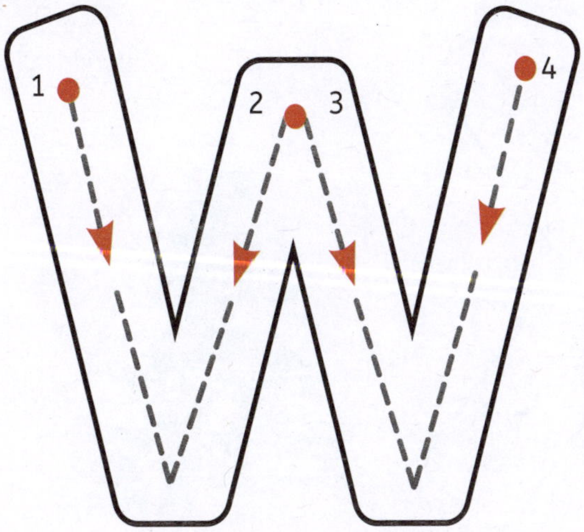

Trace

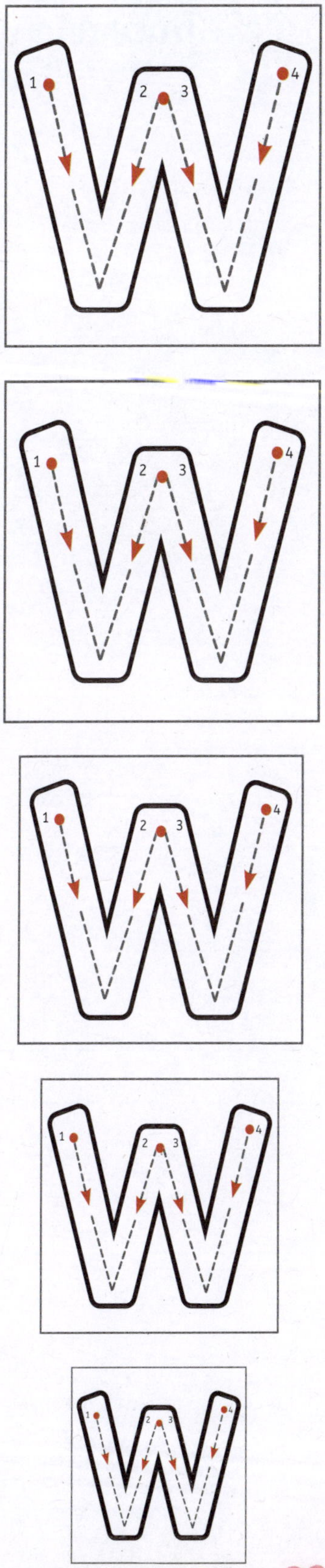

Hello Letter x

Trace and write.

Trace and write.

Hello Letter Y

Trace and write.

Trace

Hello Letter Z

Trace and write.

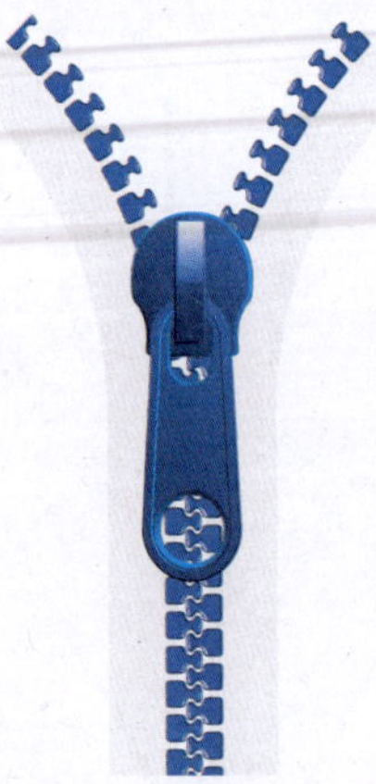

Z

Trace

I Can Write!

Trace the letters. Write them on your own.

W W

X X

Y Y

Z Z

Name the picture. Write the beginning letter.

I Can Trace Patterns!

Trace the patterns.

I Know Position Words

See the picture. Talk about the position of all the animals.

Match the animals to their positions.

between   beside   behind   on   inside   under

I Can Read Sight Words!

Point and read.

it she he boy

girl you we this

father look that am

is are first mother

Hello Letter J

Trace and write.

J

Trace

J J J J J

Hello Letter U

Trace and write.

Trace

Hello Letter B

Trace and write.

Trace

Hello Letter P

Trace and write.

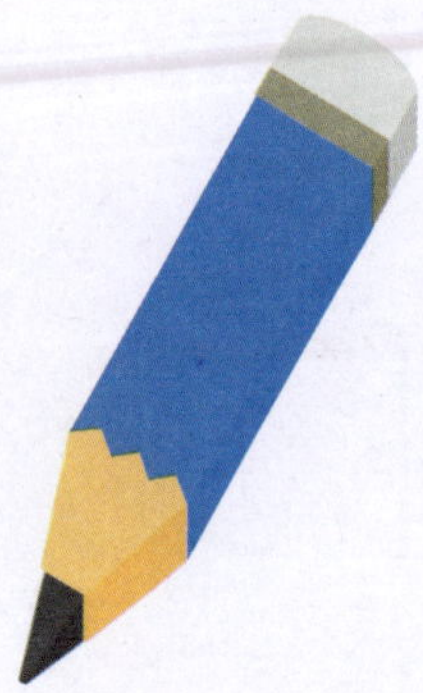

Trace

Hello Letter R

Trace and write.

R

R R R R R

R R R R R

Trace

R

R

R

R

R

I Can Write!

Trace the letters. Write them on your own.

J

U

B

P

R

I Can Trace Patterns!

Trace the patterns.

Hello Letter C

Trace and write.

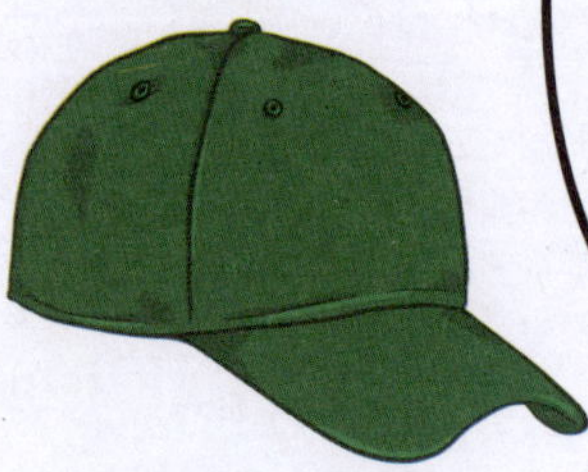

Trace

Hello Letter G

Trace and write.

Trace

Hello Letter D

Trace and write.

Trace

1 2 D

Hello Letter S

Trace and write.

Trace

Hello Letter O

Trace and write.

Trace

Hello Letter Q

Trace and write.

Trace

I Can Write!

Trace the letters. Write them on your own.

C C

G G

D D

S S

O O

Q Q

I Can Write Letters A–D

Trace and write.

A A A A

B B B B

C C C C

D D D D

I Can Write Letters E–H

Trace and write.

E E E E

F F F F

G G G G

H H H H

I Can Write Letters I–L

Trace and write.

I I I I

J J J J

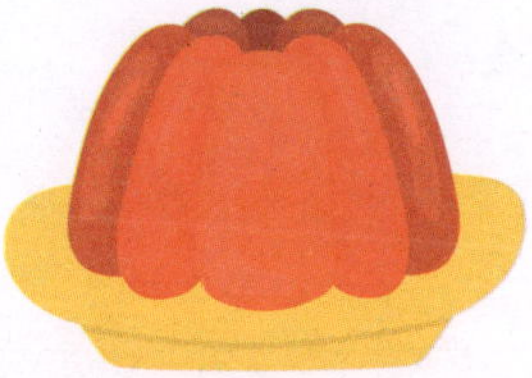

K K K K

L L L L

I Can Write Letters M–P

Trace and write.

M M M M

N N N N

O O O O

P P P P

I Can Write Letters Q–T

Trace and write.

Q Q Q Q

R R R R

S S S S

T T T T

I Can Write Letters U–Z

Trace and write.

U U

V V

W W

X X

Y Y

Z Z

I Know!

Look at the pictures. Name them. Write the first letter.

I Know!

Look at the pictures. Name them. Write the first letter.

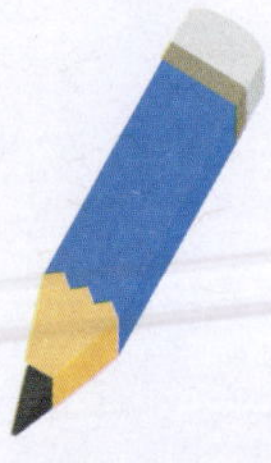

I Know!

Look at the pictures. Name them. Write the first letter.

I Can Read Words!

Match the pictures to the words.

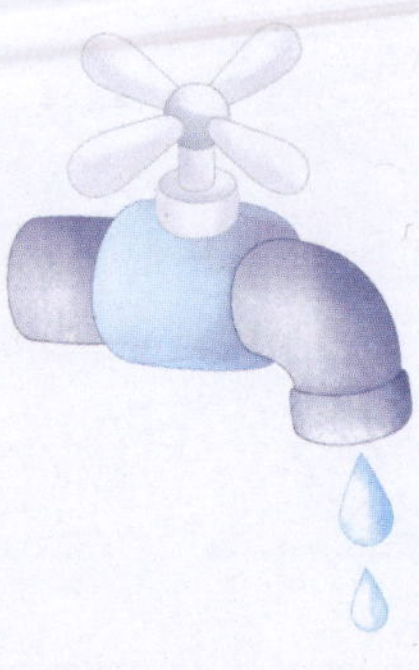

- tap
- bag
- lad
- jam
- sad
- leg
- ten
- bed
- jet

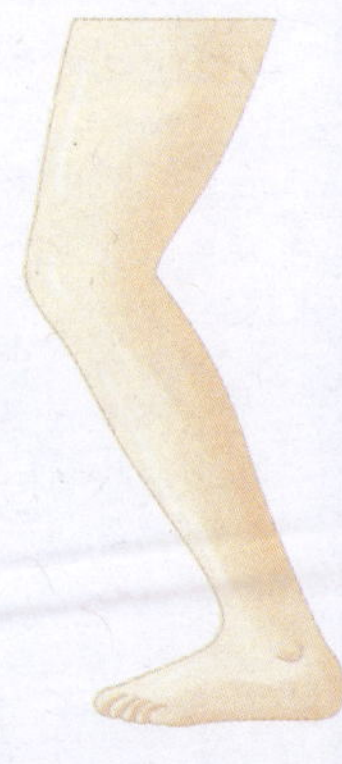

I Can Read Words!

Circle the correct word.

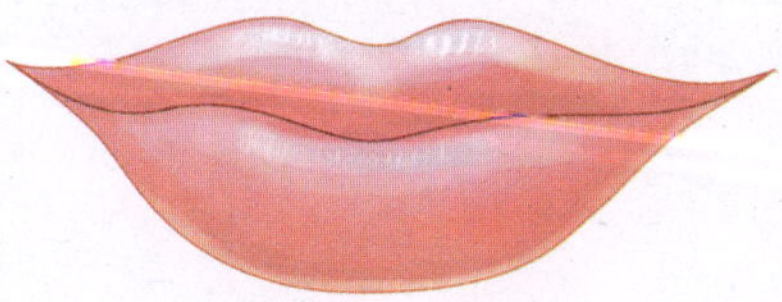

lips

dip

fit

sit

dip

sip

sit

pit

jog

fog

box

fox

hot

lot

not

pot

I Can Read Words!

Circle the correct word.

tub

pup

mug

mat

tap

sun

man

run

Cross (✗) the odd one out.

sun	bun	fun	leg
bib	lip	cot	sip
pin	pot	log	jog
dad	sad	bed	jam
leg	peg	jet	box

I Can Write!

Dip your index finger in paint. Trace the letters.

a	b	c
d	e	f
g	h	i
j	k	l
	m	

I Can Write!

Dip your index finger in paint. Trace the letters.

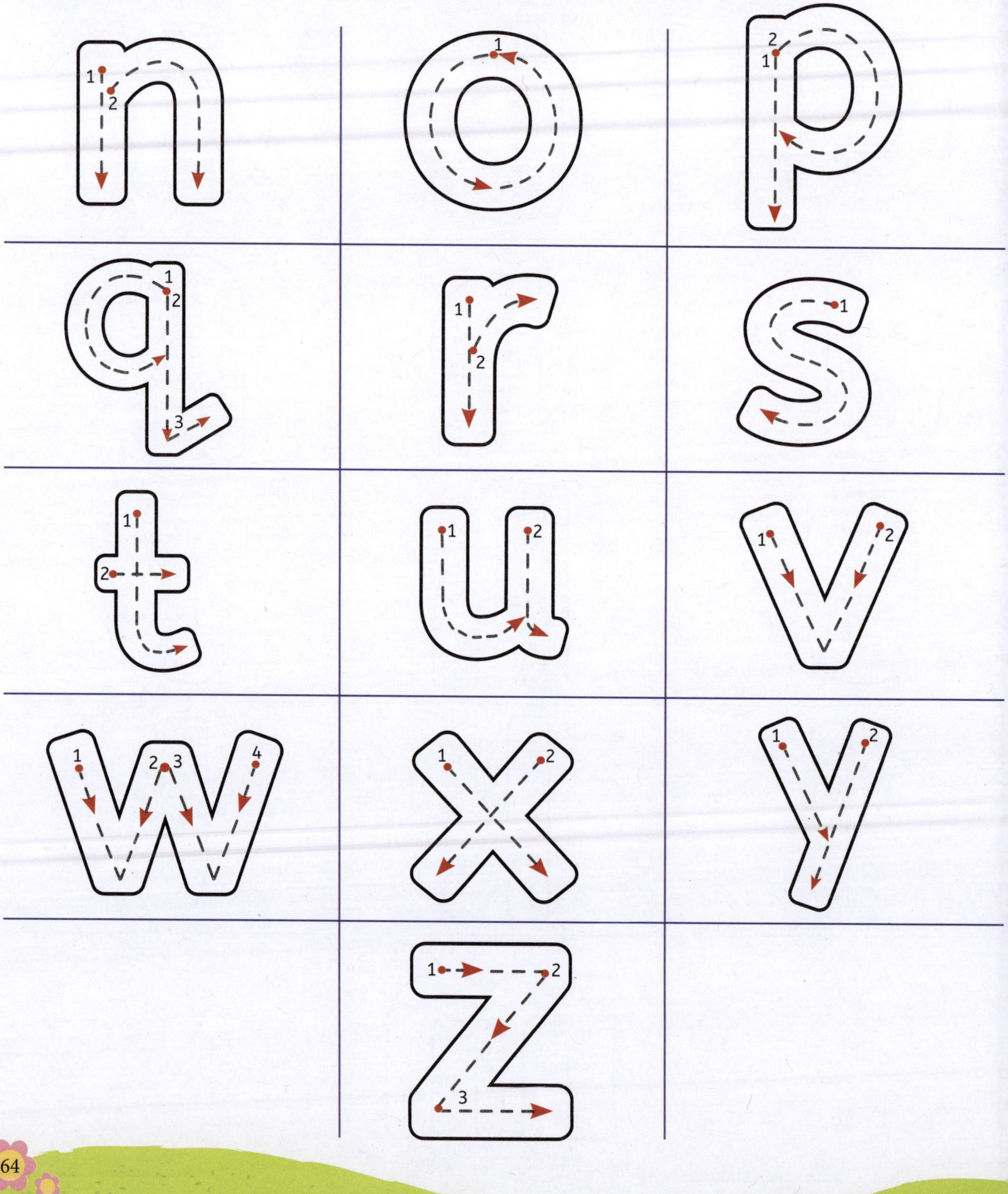